The Shining One

The Shining One

100 Things You Only *Thought* Were in the Bible

Jeffry L. Smith

2011

Parson's Porch Books   Cleveland, Tennessee

Parson's Porch Books
121 Holly Trail Road, NW
Cleveland, Tennessee 37311

The Shining One © 2011 by Jeffry L. Smith. All rights reserved.
Published 2011.
Printed in the United States of America.
ISBN 978-0982-9413-8-6

The author guarantees that all content is original and does not infringe upon the legal rights of any other person or work. No part of this book may be reproduced or transmitted in any form or by any means, electronic or mechanical, including photocopying, recording, or by information storage and retrieval system, without permission in writing from the author. The views and opinions expressed in this book are solely those of the author and do not necessarily represent those of the publisher or Parson's Porch Books.

Unless otherwise noted, scripture quotations are from the New King James Version of the Bible (© 1979 Thomas Nelson), the New Living Translation (© 1996 Tyndale House), and the Amplified Bible (© 1974 Zondervan).

To order additional copies of this book, contact:

Parson's Porch Books
1-423-475-7308
www.parsonsporch.com

TITLE PAGE ART: ADAPTED FROM WILLIAM BLAKE, *LUCIFER IN HIS ORIGINAL GLORY* (C. 1805, AFTER JOHN MILTON). ORIGINAL IN THE TATE GALLERY COLLECTION, LONDON, ENGLAND. TITLE PAGE ART, BOOK, AND COVER DESIGNED FOR PARSON'S PORCH BOOKS BY ERIC KILLINGER AT *Ars Intermundia Expressus*.

PREFACE

Having taught Church History and observed so many instances of hairsplitting and wrangling among Christians over doctrinal points that divide brothers and sisters in Christ from each other, the last thing I want to do is to add to the problem. My purpose in writing this book is to point out some interesting things that I have noted over the years.

All of us live with misconceptions. Many of them were taught to us as we sat on our little painted chairs in Sunday School. Many of them came to us in sermons. My burden is to shed some light on many of those misconceptions. My hope is to do it in a way that is neither pedantic nor preachy. Coming across as a know-it-all is the last thing I want. And, since most of the items below came as surprises to me too, I hope they will be pleasant surprises to you as well. One last thought: when you share your surprises with others, be gentle. Use phrases like, "Want to hear something I just learned?" Please, do not insult your friends and relatives by contradicting them. 2 Timothy 2:25 reminds us to "correct gently".

ACKNOWLEDGEMENTS

No one writes a book in a vacuum. Gratitude is due to all who contributed to this manuscript: my wife, RaNae, Maureen Smith, Dr. Karen Dolnick, Clarence Guthrie, and Dr. John Eric Killinger. And also, to the many Bible college students who made suggestions of things they had always thought were in the Bible, but weren't.

CONTENTS

Preface	v
Chapter One: Things You Only *Thought* Were in the Bible	1
Chapter Two: The Shining One	55
Chapter Three: So, Who Did Create Satan?	65
Chapter Four: Jesus as Seen from a Different Perspective	71
Chapter Five: Did Paul "Lose It" in Galatians 5:12?	77
Chapter Six: Did Paul Write the Book of Hebrews?	85
Chapter Seven: What Was Paul's Thorn in the Flesh?	91
Chapter Eight: Final Thought	95
Appendix	101

CHAPTER ONE

THINGS YOU ONLY *THOUGHT* WERE IN THE BIBLE

Take a moment, and see if you can determine what is common to all of these items:

1. Absolution
2. Adam and Eve ate an apple
3. Angels sing
4. Angels have wings
5. Anglicized Names: James, Judas, Mary, Simon, and Jesus
6. The Assumption of Mary
7. Balance
8. Baptism of/in/with the Holy Spirit/Ghost
9. The Beatitudes
10. The Bible
11. The camel through the Eye of the Needle refers to a gate

12. Charismatic or Pentecostal
13. Christianity
14. Christmas
15. Cleanliness is next to Godliness
16. Clergy/Laity
17. Cross
18. Curse God and die (said by Job's wife)
19. David was a little boy when he slew Goliath
20. Demon possession
21. Denomination
22. Divine healing
23. Dispensation
24. A literal dove descended on Jesus at his baptism
25. Easter
26. Ecumenical
27. Entire sanctification
28. Eternal security
29. Evangelical/Evangelism/Evangelistic
30. The Fall
31. Fallen world
32. Free Will
33. Fundamental(ism)
34. The Gift of Healing
35. God helps those who help themselves
36. God works in mysterious ways
37. The Golden Calf
38. Good Friday
39. The Good Samaritan
40. Immaculate conception
41. Incarnation
42. Infallibility/inerrancy of scripture
43. Jesus: His primary mission was to die on the cross
44. Jesus came to save souls
45. Jesus was in Hell before his resurrection

46. Jonah was swallowed by a whale
47. King David had red hair
48. The Kingdom of Heaven = Heaven
49. Kosher
50. Limbo
51. The Lord's Prayer
52. Lucifer, the archangel, became Satan
53. The mark of Cain was a punishment
54. Mary Magdalene was a prostitute
55. Millennium, pre-/post-Millennium
56. Miracles and Tongues ceased in the first century
57. Money answers all things
58. Money is the root of all evil
59. Moral: Jesus was a great moral teacher. The Bible teaches morality
60. Moses had a beard
61. Mother of God
62. Noah only took two of each animal into the ark
63. Omnipotent, omniscient, and omnipresent
64. Ordination
65. Original sin
66. Orthodox/Orthodoxy
67. Paul was in Arabia for three years
68. Paul was beheaded
69. Peter was crucified (upside down or in any position)
70. The Pearly Gates of Heaven
71. Praying with your eyes closed is the right way to pray
72. Predestination/prevenient grace
73. Pride goes before a fall
74. Prodigal Son
75. Prosperity (New Testament)
76. Pulpit, pew, nave, altar, sermon, altar call, and membership in a church

77. Purgatory
78. Rahab was an innkeeper (not a harlot)
79. The rapture
80. Revival
81. Sacrament or Sacred
82. Saul of Tarsus was knocked off of his horse on the road to Damascus
83. Second Coming
84. Seminary
85. Sermon on the Mount
86. Seven deadly sins
87. Shekhinah glory
88. I am just a sinner, saved by grace (I am only a worm)
89. The sinner's prayer
90. Spare the rod, spoil the child
91. Sword (He who lives by the sword, will die by the sword)
92. Terms: Worship leader, missionary, and reverend
93. Theology
94. The three wise men
95. Tithing reinstated in the New Testament
96. Total depravity
97. Trinity
98. Used of God
99. Wedding vows
100. Worry

Can you tell me what all the items listed above have in common? All one hundred items in the list are things often taught in Sunday school. But how many of them are actually to be found in the Bible?

I have been studying the Bible for nearly half a century, and I have noticed that there are a lot of things that are not in the Bible that we as Christians have been taught, and that we just accept as being true. As the pages to follow will show, all of the items on the list above are either (a) not to be found in the Bible, or (b) are not in the New Testament, or (c) are concepts commonly taught incorrectly.

Remember the people of Berea? (We are trying to be accurate here, so we must mention that the term "Bereans" does not occur in the Bible). The people of Berea were commended for the way they "examined the scriptures daily to see if what they had heard was true" (Acts 17:10-11). Paul commended them for this. So, let us be like them, and examine the Word of God to see what it actually says. Let us dig deeper into the mine of precious jewels that is the Bible. We need to know the Bible for ourselves, and not to just accept what we are told it says.

We, as Christians should:

> Challenge all assumptions.
> Question everything.
> Be valiant for the truth.

That's what I want to discuss in these pages: some of the things that we apparently just accept without even thinking about it. Also, we will look very deeply at one of the items in particular.

Let me preface what I am about to say with some thoughts from the Word of God. We study the scriptures, because, as Jesus said, "[We] think that in them [we] have eternal life" (Jn. 5:39)—and we do! But how do we know that we can have confidence that the Bible is the inspired Word of God in an age of higher criticism, Jesus Seminars, and rampant skepticism?

We know we can have confidence in the Bible, because if God did not convey His complete will for His children, and if every bit of the information we need to live a godly life—including the way of salvation—is not to be found between the covers of the Bible, then where else is that information to be found? And how could God judge the world for not obeying the Almighty if God failed to communicate the divine will precisely as He intends it to be obeyed? If the Bible makes an uncertain sound, to paraphrase 1 Corinthians 14:8, how would anyone know how to "prepare [oneself] for the battle?"

We can have absolute, one hundred percent trust that the God of the universe, whose power and wisdom is unlimited, inspired the words of the Bible, preserved it from error, and conveyed it to us in a form that is clear and unambiguous. We may not understand everything in the Bible—Peter calls salvation a mystery that angels desire to look into (1 Pt. 1:12). But, for most of us, as Mark Twain supposedly remarked, "It ain't those parts of the Bible that I can't understand that bother me, it's the parts that I do understand."

We need to realize that everything we need to know about God's will is in the Bible.

You will no doubt notice that throughout this book, both "Word" (when it refers to scripture or Jesus) and "Bible" are capitalized. I do so for consistency, because, as the Psalmist wrote, "You (LORD) have magnified Your Word above all Your name" (Ps. 138:2). If God has lifted up His Word even higher than His holy name, then we need to honor the Words He has given to us.

☙❧

At Christmastime we hear carols like: "Hark, the Herald Angels Sing"—and who hasn't heard how the angels sang to announce the birth of the Savior in Bethlehem? But, can you find it in the New Testament? Is there anywhere in the Bible that it says angels sing? It's not there. Anywhere. I looked. (Please, I invite you to look, too!). The Bible says angels are messengers, that they "announce," but never is it mentioned that angels "sing."

The quotation is: "And suddenly there appeared with the angel a multitude of the heavenly host praising God and *saying* . . . (Lk. 2:13). The only verse that sounds like it could possibly be interpreted to say that is in the book of Job: "the morning stars sang together" (38:7). So, if the morning stars are angels, then, okay, maybe. But it doesn't say "angels." Angels may sing very well, for all we know, but it is not stated in the Bible.

But, surely, the Bible tells us that angels have wings? Not in any way. Not anywhere. We are told that beings known as the Seraphim have wings, but they seem to be distinctly separate beings from angels (Is. 6:1-3). Cherubim, another type of heavenly being, are only mentioned in Genesis 3:24; Ezekiel 10:17–20; and 1 Kings 6:23–28. Remember, the angels that appear, for example, in the book of Genesis not only do not have wings, but they also have the appearance of human beings (Gen. 18:1-2).

What about Gabriel? No wings. Michael? No wings. In each and every appearance of angels in scripture, there is no mention of them having wings (see also, for example, Dan. 8:15 & 10:18). The only angels with wings are in religious paintings and statues.

Were there THREE WISE MEN? Well, there were three gifts, but Matthew only writes that there were "certain wise men," and does not specify how many Magi there were. Also, despite the fact that there are always three Wise Men in our nativity scenes, and despite their having been assigned arbitrary names centuries later (Caspar, Melchior, and Balthazar), the Bible indicates that they did not arrive on the night Jesus was born to see Him in the manger. Luke does not mention them at all, but Matthew's Gospel states that they arrived after the birth of Jesus (2:1), and that their visit (and the appearance of the star) involved a house, not a stable. It was probably over a year after His birth—as indicated by Herod having ordered all children under the age of two years old to be slain.

My attention was first drawn to all those things we assume are true because we have always heard them taught, when I was having a conversation with my father and said something like, "On his way to Damascus SAUL FELL FROM HIS HORSE to the ground, as a bright light shone around him." My father, who was a Bible teacher for many decades, asked me: "Can you show me that in the Bible?" I confidently turned to Acts 9, and prepared to show him. I could not believe my eyes! It wasn't there! Thinking it must have been redacted by a modern translator, I went to my Greek New Testament. Hmm . . . not there either. Yet I had a clear picture in my mind of Saul with a horse (or a donkey). I knew it was in there!

Psychologists call that false memory, or episodic amnesia. Ask any of the men who were released from jail after DNA evidence proved their innocence, who had been confidently identified by eyewitnesses as guilty. Our minds tend to fill in blanks, and, unfortunately, our memories are not like video cameras. Images change and can be influenced in a number of ways. In this case, I had been influenced by one of those religious paintings I just mentioned a few paragraphs back.

There are several well known paintings of Saul on the road to Damascus that include horses and seem to show him lying where he fell off of his horse. Combine that with many sermons and conversations that describe Saul being "knocked off of his donkey," and the image is planted. Despite the fact that I had read that passage dozens or hundreds of times, I never noticed there was no horse mentioned.

Petty? Not important? Perhaps. But let's keep going and see what else we only think is found in the pages of Scripture.

How about that APPLE Adam and Eve took from the tree? No? the book of Genesis just says "fruit."

Now, before we move on to the next section, I would like to share a brief story from the life of the Swiss reformer, Huldrich Zwingli. Zwingli wanted to restore the Church back to the model of the first century, but, unlike Martin Luther who believed anything not prohibited by the Bible was okay, Zwingli suppressed the use of musical instruments such as organs in church worship because they were not mentioned in the Bible. He even banned violins for the same reason, although he himself was a very good violinist. This is one of the reasons the Bible reminds us, "the letter kills, but the Spirit gives life" (2 Cor. 3:6).

Many of the early reformers were very strict about what they considered "biblical"—if they couldn't find it in the Bible, then we shouldn't be doing it. Taken to the extreme this can lead to many absurdities: since seat belts aren't mentioned, we shouldn't wear them; those with emphysema shouldn't use oxygen tanks (not mentioned either); no anesthesia mentioned in the Bible so operations would have to be conducted without them; etc. Again, my purpose is to point out things that are taught as if they were in the Bible but aren't—just so we know what is true and what isn't—not to produce a new list of prohibitions.

※

Now that I have your attention, let's go through the remaining items on the list, one by one:

1. ABSOLUTION

"Absolution" is a word that does not appear in Protestant translations of the Bible and denotes being *absolved* of sin. Since this term refers to a Roman Catholic rite of conciliation, a better word to use is "forgiveness."

2. ADAM AND EVE AND THE APPLE (See p. 11)

3. ANGELS SING (See p. 9)

4. ANGELS HAVE WINGS (See p. 9)

5. ANGLICIZED NAMES: JAMES, MARY, SIMON, JUDAS, AND JESUS

Interesting: During the time of the translation of the Bible into English, the translators decided to change several of the names in the New Testament that clearly occur in the Old Testament such as Jacob, Miriam, Simeon, Judah, and Joshua into Anglicized versions.

Hence:

- The name "Jacob" was translated into English, becoming "James." See Mt. 1:2, 22:32, passim, where the same Greek word is translated "Jacob" in reference to Jacob the son of Isaac—the same name that is elsewhere arbitrarily translated "James." (Greek: Ιακωβ, Ιακωβος).
- "Miriam" became "Mary" (Greek: Μιριαμ→Μαρια).
- "Simeon" (Συμεων) became "Simon" (Σιμων).
- "Judah" became "Judas" (Ιουδας)
- "Joshua" became "Jesus" (Ιησους). Three times in the New Testament the name *Iaysous* is used when describing Joshua the son of Nun from the Old Testament. The name is exactly the same as "Jesus" in Matthew 1:21, thus, when the angel said, "You shall call His name Jesus (Joshua)," Joseph (and others) would have heard and recognized the name as "Joshua" and identified it with the successor of Moses.

On a personal note, I think that the translators should have kept the names the same. It would have made for a much more seamless transition between the Old Testament and the New Testament if they had been consistent, and would have allowed Hebrew speakers to see the connection between the two.

6. THE ASSUMPTION OF THE DIVINE BLESSED VIRGIN MARY

First mentioned in the fifth century, the Assumption of the Divine Blessed Virgin Mary was proclaimed an "infallible" doctrine of the Roman Catholic Church in 1950, holding that the Virgin Mary was taken up, body and soul, into heaven in the same way that Jesus was, and did not die.

7. BALANCE

Many a sermon has been preached and much advice given on how important it is to be in "balance." We are admonished not to put too much emphasis on either the Word or the Spirit, be too zealous or too sedate, etc. But in Revelation 3:15-16, Christ tells the church at Laodicea that being balanced is displeasing to Him: "because you are lukewarm, and neither cold nor hot, I will vomit you out of My mouth." The Bible does not contain the concept of "balance" as it is commonly taught today. Jesus taught: Love God with all your heart, hate your mother, father, wife, and leave everything, or you cannot be My disciple—these are not "balanced" concepts.

8. BAPTISM OF/IN/WITH THE HOLY SPIRIT/GHOST

The word baptism is not found in this context. When people are spoken of as having been baptized in the Holy Spirit (Mk. 1:8), receiving the Holy Spirit (Jn. 20:22), or being filled with the Holy Spirit (Acts 2:4), it appears to be different ways of saying the same thing—but the Bible does not use the noun "baptism" in conjunction with the Holy Spirit. Rather, it uses the word in conjunction with phrases such as "into [Christ's] death" (Rom. 6:4), for example.

9. THE BEATITUDES

This term is not found in the New Testament, but is a designation for the portion of the sermon cited by Matthew in the fifth chapter for those sayings of Jesus that begin with the phrase, "Blessed are. . . ." The term comes from a translation of the Latin word for "blessed" *beatus*; hence, beatitude, the state of being blessed.

10. BIBLE

The word comes from *biblos* (βιβλος), which means book, but the Bible never calls itself the Bible. Peter, in describing Paul's writings in 2 Peter 3:16 states that "the untaught and unstable distort" Paul's letters "as they do also the rest of the Scriptures"—describing the Old Testament and at least some of the New Testament as "Scriptures," or "writings," but the word "Bible" is never used (in English, anyway).

11. THE CAMEL AND THE EYE OF A NEEDLE REFER TO A GATE

Since the ninth century, many a preacher has trotted out the old sermon illustration that there is a small gate in Jerusalem known as the "Eye of a Needle" and that if a laden camel kneels and sheds its goods, it can pass through the "eye of the needle" and enter in to the city. This is told to explain this parable of Jesus: "Again, I say to you, it is easier for a camel to pass through the eye of a needle than for a rich man to enter the kingdom of heaven" (Mt. 19:24). In fact there is no record of there ever having been any such gate, and the metaphor Jesus uses is just that: a way to show how difficult it is for a self-reliant person who is focused on the riches of this world to enter into God's kingdom, a kingdom that requires complete dependence on God. And, Jesus modified it, by saying, that with God, all things are possible (v. 26)—that even a rich man, with God's help, might be able to enter into the kingdom. In fact, this expression has existed in many forms for centuries before Jesus—in the Babylonian Talmud, for example, Jews used the idiom, "an elephant passing through the eye of a needle" as a way of expressing an impossibility.

Another variation on the theme, is to try and explain the parable by introducing the possibility of an error in the original Greek, based on the similarity between the two Greek words: 1. *kamilos* (camel) and 2. *kamelos* (cable, or rope), and thus, it would be easier to for a rope to go through the eye of a needle (as opposed to a thread) than for a rich man to enter the kingdom. But, since, only one or two New Testament manuscripts (and not the other 3,000 or more better copies) have that misprint, it seems to be an unnecessary explanation.

12. CHARISMATIC OR PENTECOSTAL

These terms were coined in the 20th century to describe persons who practice the gifts of the Spirit mentioned in many passages, but notably in 1 Corinthians 12. The former word derives from the Greek word *charisma* which means "spiritual gift," "a freely given gift involving grace" or just "gift," whereby the latter word is a permutation of "Pentecost" and refers to Acts 2 which describes the Holy Spirit being poured out on the church.

13. CHRISTIANITY/CHRISTENDOM

These terms originated in the fourteenth century, and were applied to Christians to describe their religion. The term "Christian," meaning "belonging to Christ" was first applied in Antioch (Acts 11:26), and is also found in Acts 26:28 and 1 Peter 4:16.

14. CHRISTMAS

Derived from the term for the Mass held for Christ's birth (Christ's Mass), it is not found in the Bible, and was first used in 1038 in England. I have always thought that if it were important for us to know when Jesus was born, we would have been told, "Celebrate My birthday on (date)." Scholarly research has shown Jesus could not have been born in winter, (no sheep or shepherds would have been in the field) and, for what it is worth, my own calculations place his birth at midnight on August 22.

15. CLEANLINESS IS NEXT TO GODLINESS

This is not a phrase from the Bible, and first appeared in the second century in the writings of a rabbi. It first appeared in English in the writings of philosopher Francis Bacon and was rephrased two centuries later by John Wesley and used in his sermons.

16. CLERIC/LAITY

There is no hierarchy in leadership other than apostle, prophet, pastor, teacher, evangelist (with overseer, deacon, and elder possibly included). No Popes, no Cardinals, no priests—no hint in the New Testament of a differentiation between those who are "approved" to preach and those who share their faith while on the job or during a normal workday. (See also ORDAINED)

17. THE CROSS

The Greek word used by Jesus when referring to that upon which He would die, and that which we as disciples need to take up daily, is "stauron"—and is best translated, "a stake or post." Many scholars have noted that the shape of the symbol does not match the shape of the type of cross that may have been used—more like a capital "T" than a † (stake and crossbar). Early Christians preferred to use the symbol of the ICThUS (Greek for "fish," denoting: *Iasous Christos Theou Huiou Soter* = Jesus Christ Son of God Savior), rather than the modern cross symbol as we know it. The use of the term "cross" in reference to the instrument upon which Christ died was not introduced into English until the middle of the tenth century AD.

18. CURSE GOD AND DIE (said by Job's wife [Job 2:9])

The Hebrew word translated "curse" is the word for an oath (baruch, as in *Baruch atah adonai* = blessed be God), and can mean either to bless or to curse. So, perhaps Job's wife was saying, "Bless the name of God, and die." Get it over with. Give up.

19. DAVID WAS A LITTLE BOY WHEN HE SLEW GOLIATH

Scripture indicates that David was at least in his twenties, despite all the Sunday school drawings and flannel boards showing a very small young boy armed with a slingshot squaring off with the giant. Most commentaries state that David was either a teenager or in his early twenties, based on the clues found in the Bible, as well as the fact that he could not have killed a bear and a lion, nor could he have picked up Goliath's sword, much less beheaded the giant with it if he were the eight-year-old often depicted. King Saul (who was a head taller than other men of Israel) would surely never have suggested putting his armor on a little boy.

20. DEMON POSSESSION

These words are used by several English translations (KJV, NKJV, NIV), but my reason for dealing with it here is to point out a distinction. Many scholars do not think "possession" is an accurate translation or description of the Greek word used to describe those who have been afflicted by demons in Matthew and Mark. The word is *daimonizomenos* (δαιμονιζομενος) and is properly translated "demonized" (Rotherham); "under the power of demons" (Amplified Bible); and "demoniacs" (NRSV).

The meaning of the word *daimonizomenos* is: to be under the influence of an evil spirit, but to say that a person is "possessed" by a demon implies that the person has lost all volition, and that their will has been completely taken over by the demon(s). While I suppose it may be possible for a person to be completely possessed by a demon and appear to be capable of functioning, several persons mentioned in the Bible who were influenced strongly by demons remained in control of their will: King Saul was troubled by an evil spirit, but was still rational and capable of functioning as a human being; the boy out of whom Jesus cast a demon in Matthew 17:15-18 only fell into the fire or water "often" (not constantly) which may indicate that the condition came and went. Those who operate in deliverance ministries say that there are many persons from whom a demon was cast out, who were unaware that they had even come under the influence of an evil spirit, even including—and I know this will be controversial—Christians.

A good analogy is found in the Book of Nehemiah. The Temple of God is like a human in this respect: there is the Outer Court, the Holy Place, and the Holy of Holies, and Christians are called the "temple of the Holy Spirit" in 1 Corinthians 3:16 and 6:19 which may correspond to body, soul, and spirit. I do not believe that a demon can possess the core spirit of a Christian, that is, enter the place where the Holy Spirit dwells. But as in Nehemiah 13:7-9, an evil being can dwell in an outer area of the Temple. Nehemiah heard of what:

> the evil Eliashib had done for Tobiah, by preparing a room for him in the courts of the house of God. It was very displeasing to me, so I threw all of Tobiah's household goods out of the room. Then I gave an order and they cleansed the rooms; and I returned there the utensils of the house of God with the grain offerings and the frankincense.

Can a Christian have a demon? Jack Hayford says, "A Christian can have anything they want, but: why would they want one?" I don't think a Christian can be "possessed" because the Bible indicates that God and Satan cannot dwell together in one heart, and, as James asks (3:12) "Can a fig tree, my brethren, bear olives, or a grapevine bear figs? Thus no spring yields both salt water and fresh." But I have personally witnessed that Christians may come under demonic influence and need deliverance and healing.

21. DENOMINATION

A "denomination" is a group of Christians who have separated themselves from other Christians because of race (as did Pentecostals in the early twentieth century) or because of doctrinal differences. The word was first seen in print in the fourteenth century, and is not found in the text of any English Bible.

22. DISPENSATIONAL, DISPENSATIONALISM

Much more recent terms than DENOMINATION (q.v.), the term "dispensationalism" was coined by John Nelson Darby in the 1830s and promulgated by C. I. Scofield to describe the time periods in which God is supposed to have divided God's working in the world. It is not a term found in the Bible.

23. DIVINE HEALING

This phrase is not found in the Bible, although there are dozens of healing miracles mentioned.

24. A DOVE DESCENDED ON JESUS AT HIS BAPTISM

Matthew 3:16 relates that Jesus "saw the Spirit of God descending as a dove and lighting on Him," which sounds like a poetic description of an event that defied description. It doesn't say that a dove descended on Jesus, but seems to indicate that the Holy Spirit descended as gently as a dove, or in a way that reminded the witness of the way a dove descends. It does not say an actual dove descended on Him, although illustrations and paintings depict a literal dove (and always a white one, at that!).

25. EASTER

Of pagan derivation from around 900 AD

when the spring rite of the rebirth of the earth was adopted from either the Babylonian goddess Ishtar or proto-Germanic Austron, goddess of fertility. There may also be a connection between the terms "Easter" and "East," due to the connection with the rising of the sun. There is no formal title (or date) given to the resurrection of Jesus. Easter is not a word used in the New Testament, but, rather, Luke uses the term, "His ascension" (9:51) and the remaining New Testament uses the phrase, "His resurrection."

26. ECUMENICAL

Coined in England in 1570 from a Greek word (*oikoumenikos* = inhabitants of the world) that does not occur in the New Testament as "Ecumenical." It has come to be seen as a means of finding unity among all denominations of Christians in organizations such as the World Council of Churches, which occasionally has met with much controversy and opposition from some Christian groups.

27. ENTIRE SANCTIFICATION OR CHRISTIAN PERFECTION

These terms refer to the doctrine that teaches a second work of grace that removes the stain of original sin. It is associated with the eighteenth century teachings of the Methodist movement.

28. ETERNAL SECURITY

The term never occurs in the Bible, and the concept that once gained, salvation cannot be lost is contradicted in many verses in the Bible: John 15:2, 6; Matthew 7:19; 12:31, and 15:14; 1 John 5:16; and Hebrews 6:4-8. The term only recently appeared in the sixteenth century, in the writings of John Calvin.

Paul himself stated that he lived in hope of salvation: "But I keep under my body, and bring it into subjection: lest that by any means, when I have preached to others, I myself should be a castaway" (1 Cor. 9:27). The Greek word translated "castaway" means "disqualified," "not standing the test," "not approved," "that which does not prove itself such as it ought," "unfit for," "unproved," "spurious," or "reprobate."

Paul also said he hoped he "might by some means" be included in the resurrection of the dead (Phil 3:11). We should never presume we are pleasing to God and that God's patience is infinite. Paul, writing to saved people in the church at Corinth (1 Cor. 6:9-11) said that even Christians who practice evil deeds will not inherit the Kingdom of God. The book of James seems to indicate that saved people will do good works, not to earn salvation, but to prove that they have received God's salvation.

29. EVANGELICAL/EVANGELISM/EVANGELISTIC

The Greek word *euangelion* (good news) denotes the Gospel, and, although the word "evangelist" does occur (Acts 21:8, Eph. 4:11, and 2 Tim. 4:5), the three forms above do not, being of much later (1730 AD) origin.

30. THE FALL

Except for that season following Summer, the phrase, The Fall, as in "the fall of mankind," does not occur in the text of any English translation of the Bible.

31. FALLEN WORLD

As in, "We live in a fallen world." Not found in the text of any English translation of the Bible. It is a phrase often heard from the pulpit, but is not a scriptural concept. Adam sinned and 1 Timothy 2:14 says, "was not deceived, but the woman being deceived, fell into transgression." Paul writes that the creation was "subjected to futility" by God (Rom. 8:20), but not that the world is "fallen."

32. FREE WILL

The words randomly come together without any reference to the doctrine of humans having "free will" in Philemon 1:14, but, other than that, the words "Free Will" do not occur in the Bible.

33. FUNDAMENTAL, FUNDAMENTALISM

First appears in the 1910s in America to describe certain groups of Christians who held to the "fundamentals" of the faith, and who opposed the "modernists" that espoused such ideas as Darwin's theory of evolution.

34. THE GIFT OF HEALING

Although Paul speaks of "gifts of healings" (1 Cor. 12:9—in the original Greek both words are plural), there does not appear to be a "gift of healing" per se, leading to the conclusion that, although God sends gifts of healings through certain persons more often than others, it is not correct to speak of the gift of healing. No one, including Jesus, healed every one of all diseases, on every occasion.

35. GOD HELPS THOSE WHO HELP THEMSELVES

A quote attributed to Benjamin Franklin and possibly originating from Aesop's fable, "The Ox-herder and Herakles," but nowhere to be found in the Bible.

36. GOD WORKS IN MYSTERIOUS WAYS

This is the title of a hymn written by William Cowper, but the phrase does not occur in the Bible.

37. GOLDEN CALF

The Bible uses the term a "molten calf" and

indicates it was made of gold. The actual term "golden calf" is never used.

38. GOOD FRIDAY

The words used to describe how long Jesus would be in the grave (three days and three nights) seem to preclude Jesus having been crucified on a Friday, since Sunday, the first day of the week (Mt. 28:1, passim) would only have been two full days and two full nights later. Hence, the term Good Friday is wrong on both counts—it was neither "good" nor was it Friday.

The term "Sabbath" is often applied to various holy days occurring on any day of the week, and since "that Sabbath was a high day" (Jn. 19:31) that forced the breaking of the prisoners legs, the crucifixion must have occurred on the Thursday Sabbath Day that preceded the Passover, and thus Jesus rose on Sunday, the "first day of the week" (Jn. 20:1)—three full days and three full nights later.

39. THE GOOD SAMARITAN

Like "the prodigal son," the words "good Samaritan" are not to be found in the story in Luke 10:33; rather, we are told about "a Samaritan who was on a journey...." His actions might have been good, but he is not spoken of as being "The Good Samaritan" (except in the headings that were added later).

40. IMMACULATE CONCEPTION

This is a term that came to be formally part of Roman Catholic Church doctrine in 1854 (the Immaculate Conception of the Divine Blessed Virgin Mary) and describes its belief that Mary was conceived without original sin.

41. INCARNATION

Yes, the Word did become flesh (Jn. 1:14)—but the word "incarnation" is not to be found in the Bible.

42. INFALLIBILITY OR INERRANCY (OF SCRIPTURE)

Though the Bible declares that "Heaven and earth will pass away, but My words will not pass away" (Mt. 5:18), the words "infallibility" or "inerrancy" are never used in reference to the Bible. There are no copyist errors in the earliest Hebrew or Greek manuscripts that affect any major doctrines, however, and we can be assured we have the Word of God as God inspired It, as holy men wrote It, and can have confidence in its accuracy.

43. JESUS: HIS PRIMARY MISSION WAS TO DIE ON THE CROSS

Jesus was the Lamb, slain from the foundation of the world, but his mission is defined in Hebrews 10:7: "Behold, I have come—in the volume of the book it is written of Me—to do your will, O God." Jesus came to do the will of the Father—dying on the cross was only part of the Father's will.

44. JESUS CAME TO SAVE SOULS

To be precise, salvation is about saving (*sōzo* = healing) the whole person—body, soul, and spirit. "Saving souls" is modern terminology.

45. JESUS WAS IN HELL BEFORE HIS RESURRECTION

This is a controversial one. There is no verse that states Jesus was ever in hell. It comes from the so called "Apostles Creed," written a century after the time of the apostles, which contains a phrase that states Jesus: "descended into hell"—from an extrapolation that many see as unwarranted from 1 Peter 3:18-20 and Colossians 2:13-15. Did Jesus go to the grave? Yes. The concept of the grave in Hebrew is Sheol. The concept in the New Testament is Hades, the place of the dead that also includes Paradise. So, the spirit of Jesus did not go to "Hell," the place reserved for the Devil and his angels (2 Pet. 2:4; Mt. 25:41), but His Spirit awaited the resurrection of his body and His ascension, in the place known as Sheol, the place of the dead described in Luke 16:19-31 and 23:43.

46. JONAH WAS SWALLOWED BY A WHALE

Nope. "The LORD appointed a great fish to

swallow Jonah" (Jon. 1:17). Not a whale, but a fish: the Hebrew word used here is, as is the word in Greek used in Matthew 12:40 when Jesus speaks of Jonah "in the belly of a great fish" (Hebrew *dag gadol* = big fish). Since marine biologists have eliminated every known form of fish or whale from being capable of swallowing a man whole, and since there would not be enough oxygen to sustain a man for three days inside any known sea creature, we are left to accept what the Bible says: that God prepared a great fish just for Jonah.

47. KING DAVID HAD RED HAIR

The Bible merely states (1 Sam. 16:12 and 1 Sam. 17:42) that David was "ruddy," which probably refers to his complexion, but there is no reference to the color of his hair.

48. THE KINGDOM OF HEAVEN = HEAVEN

Often I have heard ministers use these terms interchangeably in sermons: as in, the kingdom of heaven is like . . . and then apply it to the realm of God above, when it refers to the realm of God on earth. Proof that this is true is to be found in the other Gospels that use the term Kingdom of God instead of Kingdom of Heaven. This term only occurs in the book of Matthew, and only because Matthew, as a devout Hebrew, eschews the use of the name of God, substituting "Heaven" for the name.

49. KOSHER

This is a very modern term, being less than two hundred years old, appearing first in print in the mid-eighteen hundreds, and derives from a Hebrew word meaning something that is "proper" or "fitting"—but is not used anywhere in the Bible.

50. LIMBO

The term never occurs in scripture, but is a term of uncertain origin, and is not even an official doctrine of the Roman Catholic Church.

51. THE LORD'S PRAYER

The words "Lord's Prayer" are not found in the Bible. In Luke 11:1, the disciples of Jesus say to Him, "Lord, teach us to pray . . ." and Jesus gives them a template that should perhaps more appropriately be called the Disciples' Prayer, since He would never pray asking God to "forgive us our trespasses," having never committed any!

52. LUCIFER, THE ARCHANGEL, BECAME SATAN (SEE CHAPTER 2).

53. THE MARK OF CAIN WAS A PUNISHMENT

Actually, it was quite the opposite. According to Genesis 5:15, "the LORD set a mark on Cain, lest anyone finding him should kill him."

54. MARY MAGDALENE WAS A PROSTITUTE

Nope. The New Testament describes several women named Mary (scholars list at least six), but all that is said about Mary Magdalene is that she had seven devils cast out of her, was near the tomb where Jesus had lain, and that she announced his resurrection—no mention of prostitution.

55. PRE-MILLENNIUM, POST-MILLENNIUM

There is a period of "1,000 years" mentioned in Revelation 20:2-7, but the word "millennium" is not used in the Bible.

56. MIRACLES AND TONGUES CEASED IN THE FIRST CENTURY

Although this is even taught by some SEMINARIES (q.v.) this teaching is not Biblical. On the day of Pentecost Peter said of the outpouring of the Holy Spirit and the resulting glossolalia, "For the promise is to you and to your children, and to all who are afar off, as many as the Lord our God will call." No mention of any expiration date. In the face of multiplied millions of practicing Pentecostals and Charismatics worldwide, it is not possible for an honest observer to deny that these gifts are still operating in the Church.

Paul told the Corinthian church: "My speech and my preaching were not with persuasive words of human wisdom, but in demonstration of the Spirit and of power, that your faith should not be in the wisdom of men but in the power of God" (1 Cor. 2:4-5)—which very much sounds like a universal principle—that our faith is to be in the power of God as demonstrated by the Holy Spirit. Paul further stated that if people in church were to interpret a message in tongues, it would be such a powerful witness that unbelievers would fall down and say that truly, God is in your midst.

57. MONEY ANSWERS ALL THINGS

This verse (Eccl. 10:19) is often quoted by the prosperity teachers to justify making money the focus. But this is taking the phrase out of context: it refers back to verse 18, and is meant to be irony. As the commentary of Jamieson, Fausset and Brown states:

> Instead of repairing the breaches in the commonwealth (equivalent to "building"), the princes "make a feast for laughter (Eccl. 10:16), and wine makes their *life* glad (Ps. 104:15), and (but) money supplieth (answereth their wishes by supplying) all things," that is, they take bribes to support *their extravagance*; and hence arise the wrongs that are perpetrated (Eccl. 10:5, 6; 3:16; Is. 1:23; 5:23). MAURER takes "all things" of *the wrongs* to which princes are instigated by "money"; for example, the heavy taxes, which were the occasion of Rehoboam losing ten tribes (1 Kgs. 12:4, &c.).

58. MONEY IS THE ROOT OF ALL EVIL

What the Bible says (1 Tim. 6:10) is that "For the love of money is a root of all kinds of evil, for which some have strayed from the faith in their greediness, and pierced themselves through with many sorrows"—indicating (a) that there are other roots of evil out there; and (b) it is the love of money, not money itself that is the source of much evil.

59. MORAL; JESUS WAS A GREAT MORAL TEACHER; THE BIBLE TEACHES MORALITY

Most people who try to label Jesus as a "great moral teacher" are trying to downplay His deity. If they can make Him just one of many great teachers along with Mohammed, Buddha, Socrates, etc., then they have nullified His claim to being the Son of God. C. S. Lewis put it best:

> I am trying here to prevent anyone saying the really foolish thing that people often say about Him: "I'm ready to accept Jesus as a great moral teacher, but I don't accept his claim to be God." That is the one thing we must not say. A man who was merely a man and said the sort of things Jesus said would not be a great moral teacher. He would either be a lunatic—on the level with the man who says he is a poached egg—or else he would be the Devil of Hell. You must make your choice. Either this man was, and is, the Son of God: or else a madman or something worse. You can shut him up for a fool, you can spit at him and kill him as a demon; or you can fall at his feet and call him

Lord and God. But let us not come with any patronizing nonsense about his being a great human teacher. He has not left that open to us. He did not intend to.[1]

And, by the same token, the Bible isn't per se about "morality"—it is about holiness. "Be holy for I am holy." Being holy is infinitely above being moral. Only God can make us holy. Many have kept a moral code by willpower, but it is impossible for a human being to be pleasing to God apart from the Blood Atonement.

60. MOSES'S BEARD

Moses is always shown having a beard in artistic renditions, but that is never stated in the Bible. In fact, there are very few, if any, descriptions of the personal appearance of people to be found in the Bible.

61. MOTHER OF GOD

A common phrase among Roman Catholics, but not found in the Bible. How could a human being, created by God be the mother of God? Mary was the mother of the Son of God.

62. NOAH TOOK TWO OF EVERY ANIMAL INTO THE ARK

Noah did take at least two of every animal into the ark, but of those God called "clean," Noah took seven.

63. OMNIPOTENT, OMNISCIENT, OMNIPRESENT

Although one of these terms (omnipotent) is used once in the KJV (Rev. 19:6), it is a translation of a Greek word *pantokratōr*, which means "ruler of all," rather than "all powerful" which is what omnipotent means. These three terms are not used in the vast majority of English translations. But: Is God almighty? All knowing? Everywhere present? Yes. These are theological terms, not found in the Bible.

64. ORDINATION

The concept is a fairly recent one: that unless a person has been formally declared or "ordained" to be qualified and authorized to do so, he is not a "real" minister. It is good to have accountability, and organizations should have standards for preachers, but the term is not a Biblical term. It is used in the New Testament in Acts 10:42 and 17:31, and then only to denote the one who was ordained by God—Jesus. There are, however, guidelines for the qualifications of elders, overseers, and deacons, given in Titus 3 and 1 Timothy 1.

65. ORIGINAL SIN, ANCESTRAL SIN

These terms refer to the sin of Adam and Eve, but are not to be found in the Bible.

66. ORTHODOX, ORTHODOXY

These terms are commonly used terms meaning "straight" or "right," but the term is not used in the Bible, dating as it does from the late sixteenth century.

67. PAUL WAS IN ARABIA FOR THREE YEARS

Paul wrote in Galatians 1:16-17: "I did not immediately confer with flesh and blood, nor did I go up to Jerusalem to those who were apostles before me; but I went to Arabia, and returned again to Damascus." Note the transition from verse 17 to verse 18: "Then after three years I went up to Jerusalem to see Peter, and remained with him fifteen days." It is likely that Paul is saying, "I went to Arabia, and then returned again to Damascus. Then, after having spent three years in Damascus [not Arabia], I went up to Jerusalem."

68. PAUL WAS BEHEADED

This is not stated in the Bible, and no one really knows how he died. Mention of his having been beheaded did not come from any contemporary source, and only appeared in the fourth century.

69. PETER WAS CRUCIFIED (UPSIDE DOWN, OR IN ANY POSITION)

The details of how Peter died are speculation based on a second century source. There is no mention of how Peter died in the New Testament.

70. THE PEARLY GATES OF HEAVEN

The gates (twelve in number) made of pearl are not found in heaven, but in the New Jerusalem, which comes down from heaven (Rev. 21:21). And don't expect to see St. Peter acting as gatekeeper, either!

71. PRAYING WITH YOUR EYES CLOSED IS THE RIGHT WAY TO PRAY

Actually, there is no mention of "eyes closed" in regard to prayer. Some people find it easier to concentrate, but John 17 presents Jesus praying with His eyes lifted up to heaven.

72. PREDESTINATION/PREVENIENT GRACE

Our English translations never use "predestination" in the form of a noun—in the Greek New Testament, (Gr: *proorizō* = προοριζω) only occurs as a verb: "predestined." Several versions use the word "predestined" (Acts 4:28; Rom. 8:29, 30; 1 Cor. 2:7; and Eph. 1:5) but always in a positive way: that we were chosen for salvation and an eternal inheritance, never that we were born, doomed to hell, by the choice of God. The doctrine that says God decides prior to our birth whether we will spend eternity in Heaven or in Hell is of later origin than the New Testament. And, prevenient grace (*gratia praeveniens*) is a term used by Augustine (late third and early fourth centuries) and later by Jacob Arminius and his followers, the Wesleyans.

73. PRIDE GOES BEFORE A FALL

"Pride goes before destruction, and a haughty spirit before a fall" (Prov. 16:18).

74. PRODIGAL SON

This phrase does not occur in the story commonly known by that name, but is a title that was inserted into the text to identify this story. The New King James Version does use the word "prodigal": "The younger son gathered all together, journeyed to a far country, and there wasted his possessions with prodigal living," (Lk. 15:13)—but other than the NKJV, I don't know of any other translations that use the word. It is a translation of the Greek word *asōtōs*, meaning "dissipated," not riotous or profligate (although it is made clear in the story that his lifestyle was such). The story was aimed at the Pharisees, and the main point was the elder brother's reaction, and the loving father, not the younger son.

75. PROSPERITY (NEW TESTAMENT)

Nope. Not used once in the New Testament! Sorry, televangelists. The only use of any form of the word is in 1 Corinthians 16:2: "On the first day of every week each one of you is to put aside and save, as he may prosper, so that no collections be made when I come." There is not any scriptural basis in the New Testament for "Name It And Claim It" as a doctrine.

The other usage of "prosper" is in 3 John 1:2 where the term occurs as part of John's salutation, providing almost no support upon which to base a doctrine: "Beloved, I pray that in all respects you may prosper and be in good health, just as your soul prospers." Sounds more like John was greeting them with the hope that they would at least prosper (or do as well) spiritually as they were in their earthly life. Again: nothing to do with being rich.

In fact, as a friend of mine reminded me, "The sign of God's favor in the Old Testament was prosperity. But in the New Testament, it is suffering." Don't believe me? Read 1 Peter 4:12-19. Then do a word study on "tribulation," "suffer," and "suffering" in the New Testament—and if that doesn't convince you that seeking riches will damage your life, listen to what Paul says in 1 Timothy 6:10: "For the love of money is a root of all kinds of evil, for which some have strayed from the faith in their greediness, and pierced themselves through with many sorrows."

76. PULPIT, PEW, NAVE, ALTAR, SERMON, ALTAR CALL, AND CHURCH MEMBERSHIP

These terms are all of later origin than the New Testament, and have come to be part of our everyday church services, but they were not mentioned in the New Testament in referring to the church or to church services.

77. PURGATORY

Again, not in the Bible. The first time the term "purgatory" was actually used was in the Roman Catholic Church's First Council of Lyon in 1254 and is not part of Protestant doctrine.

78. RAHAB WAS AN INNKEEPER (NOT A HARLOT)

I have heard many sermons where the speaker tried to say that Rahab, (mentioned in Josh. 49) was an innkeeper, not a harlot. She is called in Hebrew an *'ishach* and, although there is some latitude with that Hebrew word used 780 times in the Old Testament, variously translated "woman," "adulteress," and only five times as "harlot," the New Testament makes it clear (Heb. 11:31) by use of the word *pornay* (πορνη, *prostitute*) that she indeed was involved in sexually immoral conduct.

79. THE RAPTURE, THE SECRET RAPTURE, PRE-TRIB(ULATION) RAPTURE

Nope. Not once. The term "rapture" referring to a pre-millennial rapture first appeared in print in 1738 AD. The etymology of the word is that it is a transliteration of the Latin word *raptus* used in the Vulgate Bible in 1 Thessalonians 4:17 and taken from the Greek word *harpazō* ('αρπαζω), which means "caught up" or "taken away." The concept of a secret "rapture" or catching away of the church was taught by both Cotton and Increase Mather. The concept was further spread by C. I. Scofield who included dispensationalism and the rapture in his Scofield Reference Bible. Those concepts spread rapidly, especially in America. But the majority of Christian Churches worldwide do not teach a secret rapture, but rather the Second Coming of Christ and the end of the age. The Rapture is supposed to take place as a way of secretly removing the Church prior to the so-called Seven Year (or Great) Tribulation, and is believed by some to precede and to be distinct from the Second Coming of Christ which will be visible to everyone.

Jesus said that His return would be seen as lightning is seen, flashing from the East to the West—and there is nothing secret about lightning. The verses in Matthew 24, the text most commonly used to support the secret rapture, actually seem to indicate quite the opposite. The disciples ask Jesus to tell them what the sign of the end of the age would be (v. 3) and He answers, saying that just as the people in Noah's day did not know what was happening until the flood came and took them all away, so would it be in the time of His return:

> They did not understand until the flood came and took them all away; so will the coming [presence] of the Son of Man be. Then there will be two men in the field; one will be taken and one will be left. Two women will be grinding at the mill; one will be taken and one will be left.

And then in 13:30, the Master says:

> Allow both to grow together until the harvest; and in the time of the harvest I will say to the reapers, "First gather up the tares and bind them in bundles to burn them up; but gather the wheat into my barn."

Note that the wheat, not the tares are left behind. The meek are to inherit the earth—they are not evacuated. Later in the same chapter (vv. 48-50), Jesus tells us that the angels first remove out the evil, and the righteous remain.

80. REVIVAL

Not a Biblical term. English versions use the term "revive" in the sense of spiritual renewal between four (NIV) and nineteen (NKJV) times, but the term "revival" is not to be found. Theologically, it might be better to speak of renewal, since revival means "to bring back from the dead" (See ETERNAL SECURITY, p. 22).

81. SACRAMENT

This term came into usage in the twelfth century to describe a sacred rite, but the Bible never uses it.

82. SAUL OF TARSUS KNOCKED OFF HIS HORSE (see pp. 10-11)

83. SECOND COMING

This phrase does not occur in the New Testament, but the clear teaching is that Jesus will return for His bride. The Greek word used for His return is *parousia*, meaning "presence or advent."

84. SEMINARY

This term, meaning a seed plot or nursery, refers to a school of formal training for the ministry and does not occur in the Bible.

85. THE SERMON ON THE MOUNT

This is a heading used to designate a particular sermon delivered by Jesus, but it is not called the Sermon on the Mount in the Bible.

86. THE SEVEN DEADLY SINS

Nowhere does the Bible list seven deadly sins. The list—gluttony, lust, greed, sloth, wrath, envy, and pride—dates from the fourth century AD.

87. SHEKINAH GLORY

The word *shekinah* is never used either in the Old or New Testament. It is a term that did not appear in print until the mid-seventeenth century, where it was to be found in Jewish

Kabbalistic writings of the period. *Shekinah* denotes the illuminating presence of God.

88. I AM JUST A SINNER, SAVED BY GRACE/I AM ONLY A WORM

Many hymns from centuries past have, in their zeal to exalt God, portrayed our state as that of a miserable worm, a teaching that is sometimes referred to as "Worm Theology." Examples include Isaac Watts's hymn, "Alas, and Did My Savior Bleed": "Would he devote that sacred head for such a worm as I?" In the hymn "Amazing Grace," we are told that God saved "a wretch like me." While it is true that Paul considered himself to be the "chief of sinners," is it right and biblical to say, "I am just a sinner, saved by grace?" I don't think so, even if only for the reason that the word "just" signifies that is all we are.

The only references to a man being like a worm are found in the writings of suffering men, never being stated by God concerning mankind (see Job 25:4-6 and Ps. 22:6). Even in Isaiah 41:14, God portrays not how man is, but how he sees himself. Man was created in the image of God, and although that image was altered by the presence of sin, it was not eradicated. Jesus did not die for worthless, garbage-people. He loved us even though we were yet sinners, but, as a friend reminded me, "God may love you the way you are, but God has no intention of leaving you that way."

The Bible tells us that we were sinners, and that we are not to go on sinning (but if any one does sin, there is forgiveness available). Thus, since we are now a new creation, a holy people, "saints," we are not just sinners saved by grace. We are to be more than that; rather than "a guilty, weak, and helpless worm" who falls "on Thy arms" to quote Isaac Watts, we are to be as Jesus said, "Perfect as your heavenly Father is perfect." To leave us in the state of sinner, worm, or wretch, is to deny the transforming power of the resurrection.

89. SINNER'S PRAYER

The term does not occur in the Bible, and was coined in the twentieth century by evangelicals.

90. SPARE THE ROD, SPOIL THE CHILD

Actually, the verse reads, "He who spares his rod hates his son, but he who loves him disciplines him promptly" (Prov. 13:24).

91. SWORD; HE WHO LIVES BY THE SWORD, WILL DIE BY THE SWORD

The Gospel of Matthew reports that Jesus said, "All those who take up the sword shall perish by the sword" (Mt. 26:52). The distinction is that those who are police or military are not proscribed from making their living by defending others—but, rather, the context of this passage is that Peter drew his sword and took a swing at those who came to arrest Jesus, (Jn. 18:11), and Jesus told him to put it away, warning him that in this instance it would result in instant reprisals by the soldiers, a bloody fight, and the tactics of the Zealots were not his tactics. Yet, in Luke 22:36, Jesus suggests that his disciples should go out and buy a sword: "Whoever has no sword is to sell his coat and buy one!"

How can we reconcile that with Matthew 5:39, "But I say to you, do not resist an evil person; but whoever slaps you on your right cheek, turn the other to him also"?

It seems to me that that last quotation applies more to perceived offenses and insults, rather than lethal attempts by persons intent on victimizing you or another person. We live in a dangerous, fallen world, filled with all kinds of predators—some with four legs, and some with two. Jesus did not want his disciples to be helpless victims while out ministering in areas where wild animals and thieves might attack them, so He told them to arm themselves for defensive purposes.

I know of a believing Christian, who, when he was warned by a United States Forest Ranger that he needed to carry a gun because of mountain lions and grizzlies in the area where he would be hiking, said, "I don't need a gun. God will protect me." Days later, all that was found of him were his blood-soaked jeans with his New Testament still in the back pocket. We cannot presume that God will protect us from bad things, any more than we can say, "I don't need to wear a seatbelt, because God will never let me be in an accident." As Christians, we should not be presumptuous when it comes to common sense. We have life insurance, car insurance, and health insurance—not because we lack faith, but because bad things happen. It is not faith to walk around barefoot, believing God will never let you step on anything sharp . . .

While Christians are not expected to be passive and just allow evil to flourish by never defending themselves, their families, or their country from others with evil intentions, these are issues that each of us must decide for ourselves.

Notice that when Jesus was slapped on the cheek, He did not turn the other cheek! One commentary puts it this way:

> Our Lord's own meek, yet dignified bearing, when smitten rudely on the cheek (Jn. 18:22, 23), and not literally presenting the other, is the best comment on these words. It is the preparedness, after one indignity, not to invite but to submit meekly to another, without retaliation, which this strong language is meant to convey (Jamieson, Fausset, & Brown).

Another commentary notes: "Jesus does not mean that if someone hits us across the right side of our head with a baseball bat, we should allow them to then hit the left side" (Guzman).

Sometimes violence is the right response—as demonstrated when "meek and mild" Jesus grabbed a whip, threw some tables around, and drove the money changers out of the temple (Mt. 21:12)!

92. TERMS: WORSHIP LEADER, MISSIONARY, AND REVEREND

None of these three terms is ever used in the New Testament, and are fabricated constructs:

- WORSHIP LEADER

  The New Testament is clear as to what God has placed in the church: pastor, teacher, evangelist, prophet, apostle, deacon, elder, and overseer. There is not a single place in the New Testament that describes the office of "worship leader"; however, the modern church apparently thought it wise to create one and so added it to the roster. Paul suggests that when we come together, we should each of us have a Psalm. Not that there should be a person in the spotlight. I guess in a large church setting you have to have someone leading worship—but they should be facilitators, not stars. They should fade into the background of the real purpose of corporate worship, the bride and the bridegroom embracing. In other words, check your ego at the door, humble yourself, and focus on God! Unfortunately, many Americans in the United States are star struck and want to elevate musicians and singers to celebrity status. I think the Bible calls that "idolatry . . ."

- MISSIONARY

It seems that we like to coin new titles that are different from the ones in the word of God. Modern missionaries would have been called either evangelists (if they were preaching salvation) or apostles (if they were also planting churches). Paul was an apostle and is a good example of an apostle: a person containing all five gifts in one: he was sent by the Lord (apostle = sent one); he proclaimed the word of God as he heard it from God (prophet = forth teller); he oversaw the organizing and care of groups of people into churches (pastor = shepherd); he taught the word of God (teacher); and he preached salvation (evangelist = bringer of good news). A missionary might plant and water, but unless a church is established and taught, little of lasting value will be accomplished.

- REVEREND

This is a fifteenth century term that derives via French or directly from the Latin word *reverendus*, which means "to be revered." Since a minister is to be a servant and to lay down his life for the sheep, addressing your pastor with titles like: "The One to Be Revered" John Jones is not only unbiblical but is contrary to the spirit of the Jesus who came to be a servant. He said to call no man "father" because we have one Father only, and not to call anyone Rabbi: "Do not allow anyone to call you Rabbi, for One is your Teacher" (Mt. 23:8). Jesus was not big on titles or accolades, and I would imagine terms like "Your Worship," "My Lord," "Your Grace," etc., would also fall under the same condemnation.

93. THEOLOGY

Composed of two Greek words meaning "the study of God" in the early fourteenth century, this term is not found in the Bible. Any attempt by a finite mind to categorize, describe, or explain an infinite God is always a human endeavor and doomed to never capture the fullness of its subject.

94. THREE WISE MEN (see pp. 9-10)

95. TITHING (NEW TESTAMENT)

Tithing is not even mentioned in the New Testament except in Matthew 23:23, and there in reference to the Pharisees' practice of overdoing it. Personally, I believe that if tithing was practiced by the early patriarchs, and further established under Mosaic law, how much more should we who have received grace through the death and resurrection of Jesus give far beyond the minimal ten percent? But tithing was not reinstated as a command in the New Testament. I would think if it were a very important doctrine, it would have been clearly taught and reiterated by Jesus and the New Testament writers, but, nowhere is it said, "Believe, be baptized, tithe, and you shall be saved."

96. TOTAL DEPRAVITY

This term seems to be linked with Augustine (354–430 AD) but is not in the New Testament.

97. TRINITY

There are many, many verses in both the Old and New Testaments that clearly display the tri-unity of God; however the word "trinity" per se does not occur in the Bible, and the first record of the term comes from around 170 AD.

98. TO BE USED OF GOD

This phrase, and related ones such as "I want God to use me" for such and such are not biblical. God sends. God empowers. God works through us. But nowhere in the Bible does it say that God wants to "use" us. Things are used, people are fellow servants or friends of

God, as Jesus makes clear in John 15:15: although his disciples previously had been called servants, henceforth they would be called friends. To be "used of God" may be a chorus, but it is not descriptive of the character of our Lord.

99. WEDDING VOWS

Does God want men and women to live in an unmarried state? Absolutely not. The Bible states that marriage is honorable. But, nowhere in the Bible are we told that anyone exchanged vows. Yes, Jesus attended a wedding. Many weddings are mentioned in the Bible, but nowhere do we find any kind of a script for a ceremony, nor do we have any actual vows spelled out.

100. WORRY

I threw this one in as a reminder: the Bible admonishes us to "be anxious for nothing" and to "take no thought for tomorrow"—so, clearly the idea of worry is there—but the word itself does not appear.

CHAPTER TWO

THE SHINING ONE

The devil is "God's devil."

— Martin Luther
(attribtuted)

Almighty God, Himself supremely good, would never permit the existence of anything evil among His works, if He were not so omnipotent and good that He can bring good, even out of evil.

— Augustine

THE MOST ASTUTE READERS will have noticed the one item we have not yet dealt with:

52. LUCIFER, THE ARCHANGEL, BECAME SATAN.

A footnote to Isaiah 14:12-23 that I found in the Amplified Bible says it so well that I will quote it here, and then we will examine it in detail:

> The Hebrew for this expression—"light-bringer" or "shining one"—is translated *lucifer* in The Latin Vulgate, and is thus translated in the King James Version. But because of the association of that name with Satan, it is not now used in this and other translations. Some students feel that the application of the name Lucifer

to Satan, in spite of the long and confident teaching to that effect, is erroneous. The application of the name to Satan has existed since the third century AD, and is based on the supposition that Luke 10:18 is an explanation of Isaiah 14:12, which many authorities believe is not true. "Lucifer," the light-bringer, is the Latin equivalent of the Greek word "*Phōsphoros*," which is used as a title of Christ in 2 Peter 1:19 and corresponds to the name "radiant and brilliant Morning Star" in Revelation 22:16, a name Jesus called Himself. This passage here in Isaiah 14:13 clearly applies to the king of Babylon.[2]

BUT, SURELY, THERE WAS A FALLEN ANGEL NAMED LUCIFER?

Is that really what the Bible says? Are you sure? According to many commentaries, *The Interpreter's Bible*, and several lexicons, it is not. Let's take a long, in-depth look at that. Even though much of our ideas about Satan being a fallen angel derive from Milton's *Paradise Lost*, neither Milton nor the Bible use the term "fallen angel"—not even once.

In BOOK VII of *Paradise Lost*, Milton wrote:

> Th' infernal Serpent; he it was, whose guile
> Stird up with Envy and Revenge, deceiv'd
> The Mother of Mankinde, what time his Pride
> Had cast him out from Heav'n, with all his Host
> Of Rebel Angels, by whose aid aspiring
> To set himself in Glory above his Peers,
> He trusted to have equal'd the most High,
> If he oppos'd; and with ambitious aim
> Against the Throne and Monarchy of God
> Rais'd impious War in Heav'n and Battle proud
> With vain attempt. Him the Almighty Power
> Hurl'd headlong flaming from th' Ethereal Skie

> With hideous ruine and combustion down
> To bottomless perdition, there to dwell
> In Adamantine Chains and penal Fire,
> Who durst defie th' Omnipotent to Arms.
>   (See also the Appendix).

Almost every word of the above passage occurred only in Milton's imagination! Not in the Bible!

The Bible never states that Satan ever was an angel; rather, we are told in 2 Corinthians 11:14 that he *transforms himself* into an angel (of light)—not that he ever was an angel.

Many people still wish to cling to the familiar, the things with which they are comfortable. "Don't confuse me with the facts," they say, "my mind is made up!" It reminds me of the story about the man who went to a psychiatrist because he was convinced he was dead. After many sessions, the man still clung to his delusion, despite all the proofs his doctor offered. Hoping to finally break through to the man, the psychiatrist devised a solution: He gave his patient several articles from medical textbooks describing the characteristics of dead men and emphasized the fact that dead men don't bleed. When the patient returned for his next session, his doctor asked him, "Well, what did you learn from your reading?"

He answered, "Medical evidence proves that dead men don't bleed."

"Are you willing to admit that if you were to bleed, it will prove you are not dead?"

"Absolutely," said the patient.

The psychiatrist pricked his patient's finger with a pin and a drop of blood appeared. Staring at his finger and the blood, the patient cried, "Medical science is wrong! Dead men *do* bleed!"

It's not easy to see the Bible without any extra baggage. Many of us have been taught in Sunday school that Satan was originally created good—that he was an angel but fell from heaven because of pride. But, what does *the Bible* say about the origin of Satan? "Now there was a day when *the sons of God* came to present themselves before the LORD, and Satan came also among them." (Job 1:6)

Note here that there was no panic, no mad scramble to evict this being named Satan from heaven. He seemed to be quite relaxed in the presence of God, and those around him were relaxed, as well. Satan is either being described in this passage as a "son of God" or that he was merely *among* the sons of God. Either way, the Bible never states that Satan is, or was an angel—not anywhere. Neither does the encounter between Jesus and Satan, when he appeared to tempt Him in the wilderness, contain an element of surprise, fear, or panic. Jesus talked with Satan as He talked with anyone else, answering each of Satan's three temptations with scripture.

The one section of the Bible that is most often cited as proof of Satan's having existed as an unfallen being, who subsequently fell, is Isaiah 14—*but this section is clearly about a man, and Satan is a spirit, not a man.* (Jn. 13:27, Eph. 2:2). Listen, with fresh ears, to what it is really being said:

> The Lord said to Isaiah, "Take up this proverb against *the king of Babylon*, and say: The *worms cover you*. How are you fallen from heaven, *O shining one*, son of the morning! For you have said in your heart, I will ascend into heaven, I will exalt my throne above the stars of God. . . . I will ascend above the heights of the clouds; I will be like the most High. Yet you shall be brought down to hell, . . . they that see you shall say, 'Is this *the man* that made the earth to tremble, . . . you are cast out of your *grave* . . .'" (Is. 14:4, 11-17).

Let's take another look at the complete footnote from the Amplified Bible, and this time I will paraphrase it and include the actual Greek and Hebrew words. This passage is clearly describing a man, not a spirit, since spirits cannot be "covered in worms"—and only a mortal man would need a "grave."

The term "lucifer" (my note: small "l") originally translated "light-bringer" or "shining one" from the Hebrew word for "daystar" (הילל [*haylayl'*]), but because of the association of that name with Satan *it is not now used* (emphasis mine). Some students feel that the application of the name Lucifer to Satan, in spite of the long and confident teaching to that effect, is erroneous. Lucifer, the light-bringer, is the Latin equivalent of the Greek word *phōsphoros* (φωσφορος), which is used as the title of Christ in 2 Peter 1:19 and corresponds to the title Christ ascribed to Himself: "I am the bright Morning Star (φωσφορος)" (Rev. 22:16). The application of the name, Lucifer, has existed since the third century AD, and some authorities think it is not a correct application.

The passage in Isaiah 14 is clearly describing a *man* who was a king, and who, like Nebuchadnezzar, was full of pride, desired to be worshipped, and was judged for it. Yet, if you took a poll, most Christians would say that Lucifer *was* Satan. But even the Latin Bible, written seventeen centuries ago did not *capitalize* the word (it was only capitalized in later English translations), or indicate that it's a *name*: "*quomodo cecidisti de caelo lucifer*, . . . —how you have fallen from heaven, light bearer. . . ."

The Latin word is a combination of "light" (*lucis*) plus "bringer" (*fero*). Do you see? It is not a name. The Bible does not use this word "lucifer" anywhere else, nor does it apply it to Satan as a title or a name.

The second of the three passages often applied to the origin of Satan is Ezekiel 28:2 where Ezekiel is told to direct a prophecy against, again, another *king* "the king of Tyre"—who is told "you are only a man—made of earth" (v. 9). Verse 13 refers to someone who had been "in Eden, the garden of God" and in verse 14: "With an anointed guardian cherub I placed you"—a possible reference to the angel sent to guard the entrance to the Garden of Eden with a flaming sword.

It goes on: "I cast you out as a profane thing from the mountain of God, and the guardian cherub drove you out." This could apply also to Adam who was driven from Eden. Again, nothing is proved or disproved as to the origin of *Satan*.

The last passage that is used in this connection is in Revelation 12:4: "and (the dragon's) tail drew the third part of the stars of heaven, and cast them to the earth." 12:7:

Then war broke out in heaven, Michael and his angels going forth to battle with the dragon; and *the dragon and his angels* fought, but they were defeated and—[not "that angel," but] "that *serpent*, who is called the Devil and Satan, was forced out of heaven. This great dragon . . . was thrown down to the earth with all his angels."

Note—it is not an *angel* who is tempting *other* angels to follow him; it is a *dragon*—a creature very different from an angel.

What did Jesus teach about the origin of Satan? He told the Pharisees: "You are of your father the devil . . . He was a murderer from the *beginning*, and did not stand in the truth, because there is no truth in him . . ." (Jn. 8:44). *From the beginning*: the Greek (απ' αρχης [*ap' archays*]) means literally "from ancient times" or it can mean "before all time." So, is that before creation? Before Satan's creation? The earth's?

A simple solution is that we understand John 1:1, "*In the beginning* (Εν αρχη [*en archay*] was the Word" . . . to refer to an event of eternal agelessness, or we would be left with the conclusion that the Son of God, (the Word), had a beginning. The *same* word *archay* also occurs again in 1 John 3:8a "He that commits sin is of the devil; for the devil sins *from the beginning*." It does not say, "from the time he fell." Remember: Jesus said, "He was a murderer from the *beginning*— there is no truth in him. . . ."

Having just shown that *Jesus* is the shining one, the light bearer, (*luci-fer*) we will now proceed to show how the term *lucifer* came to be capitalized and identified with Satan, and where this idea originated.

The Amplified Bible says that some people have associated the following passage from Luke 10 with Isaiah 14, but the *context* of this passage has more to do with "binding the strong man" than it does with the origin of Satan. Luke wrote in verse 17: "The seventy returned with joy, saying, 'Lord, even the demons obey us when we use your name!' 'Yes,' Jesus told them, 'I saw Satan falling from heaven as a flash of lightning.'"

Is Jesus referring back to something that occurred eons before, when Satan was cast out of heaven, or is he commenting on what had just happened a few minutes before: Satan's power being broken by his disciples? Jesus seems to be saying to the disciples, "Yes, I watched the prince of the power of the air lose his power over his victims, even as you ministered! I watched as he fell from the heavens!" If Jesus was referring to Satan being cast out of heaven, I believe He would have said that plainly.

I have always wondered why many men and women of God who are in deliverance ministry have pointed out that demons, speaking through a demonized person, expressed the preference for the name "Lucifer" to any other name, when referring to Satan: could it be because these lying spirits, knowing lucifer is not a name belonging to Satan, are secretly amused by their deceit?

Whatever the passage in Luke 10 means, it is not about the origin of Satan, and simply cannot be used to prove that Satan is *lucifer*, that he was ever an angel, or that he fell.

CHAPTER THREE

SO, WHO DID CREATE SATAN?

The Bible never explains that, nor is it stated when Satan was created. The devil just appears in the first chapters of Genesis as a serpent, without any explanation. (Some scholars are unsure that the serpent of Genesis is Satan, but Revelation 12:9 seems to indicate he was).

Why do we have difficulty accepting that God created the devil? Either Satan was created as an angel and subsequently fell—for some reason that the Bible doesn't tell us about—or it is as Isaiah stated it: "Behold, I (the Lord) have created the blacksmith, blowing on the fire of coal, and bringing out a weapon for his work, and I have created the waster to be a destroyer" (Is. 54:16).

COULD A HOLY, JUST, AND LOVING GOD HAVE CREATED EVIL?

The study of how God can be good and still allow evil is called Theodicy, and these questions have been asked and discussed for many centuries. Who placed the tree of the knowledge of good and evil in the Garden (Gen. 2:9)? Satan? No.

Who takes credit for the dumb, deaf, and blind?

"And the LORD said unto [Moses], 'Who has made man's mouth? Or who makes the dumb, or the deaf, or the seeing, or the blind? Have not I, Jehovah'" (Ex. 4:11)?

Who is in control of evil spirits? In 1 Samuel 16:14 states that "an evil spirit from Jehovah" troubled King Saul.

Is Satan in charge of disasters? The Lord says in Isaiah 45:7: "I form the light, and create darkness: I make peace, and create calamity: I Jehovah do all these things."

A quick Hebrew word study: The Hebrew word used here for calamity, is *rah* and is translated variously as: "bad" (of kind, such as land or water, or of value), "unpleasant," "evil" (giving pain, unhappiness, misery), "displeasing," "worse," "sad," "unhappy," "hurtful," "unkind" (vicious in disposition), "wicked" (ethically), "distress," "misery," "injury," "calamity," "adversity," "injury," "wrong," "misery." God claims to be behind all of these evils, not Satan.

Even in the case of Job, Satan was completely under the control of God who limited what Satan could and could not do. And, don't forget who initiated the conversation that resulted in the trials of Job: "Have you considered my servant, Job?"

The Lord also gave Paul "a thorn in the flesh, a messenger of Satan to buffet" him (2 Cor. 12:7a). The word translated messenger is the Greek word angel—*angelos*, "angel or messenger."

There is a great number of passages in the Bible where God personally and specifically says God is responsible for handicaps, evil spirits, and catastrophes.

So "whence Satan," as Augustine put it (*Unde Satan*), where did Satan and evil spirits originate? All we know for sure is that there are beings that have been let loose upon the earth who are actively destructive, and who are willing "evil with a terrible energy"—"the brightest creatures bereft of light, and intent on destruction."[3]

But the Son of God has given us power over the devil, and has told us to resist him and "he will flee from you" (James 4:7). God has always kept and always will keep Satan under His control.

Remember this: "The devil is God's devil,"[4] according to Martin Luther.

There is no reason to live in fear of evil—the universe is in God's hands. The evil in the world is contained by God, though it is still among us. Evil has never ceased to be under God's sovereign control. But there is no Dualism—there is not a struggle between an evenly matched God and Satan, each grappling for control. Rather, God knows exactly what Satan will do next. He is a tool in the hand of God, completely under God's control, and Satan will never pose a threat to God's ultimate triumph.[5]

Still, we are left with questions. Why does God allow evil, and not destroy it? Where did it come from? How can God judge Satan if he is only doing what he was created to do? Why does God allow Satan to do God's will—and then throw him in the Lake of Fire (Rev. 20:10)?

Some theologians have proposed that Satan is like those who are described in (2 Pet. 2:12): "they are like beasts who are only born to be killed." If Satan is not an angel, what order of creation is he? It seems to be one of those mysteries God has not chosen to tell us. But if Satan never was an angel, we certainly should never "transform him into an angel of light." And if he never was a beautiful, glorious, shining creature, then let us no longer speak of him that way.

When compared to the sovereignty, power, and wisdom of God, Satan is nothing. God has created Satan and uses him for a good purpose. Remember the quotation from Augustine with which we began this chapter? "Almighty God, Himself supremely good, would never permit the existence of anything evil among His works, if He were not so omnipotent and good that He can bring good, even out of evil."[6]

We must have such an exalted view of God that God dwarfs evil with overwhelming greatness. God is so big, that God can create good and evil, encompass them both, and still remain holy and pure. God reigns.

Let's be like the people of Berea and challenge *ALL* assumptions

CHAPTER FOUR

JESUS AS SEEN FROM A DIFFERENT PERSPECTIVE

I F A NEWSPAPER REPORTER were to view the life of Jesus just from outward appearances, it might look something like this:

> He was born in one country, raised in another for several years. His father was twenty years older than his mother, and he had several brothers and sisters. His mother, who had gotten pregnant out of wedlock, was a teenager when he was born. Rumors and nasty comments swirled around him all his life as people speculated as to who his real father might be. He became very close to his mother, as his father disappeared early on. He grew up practicing one faith but soon began modifying its tenets. He worked and lived among lower class people as a young adult, had no formal education, and worked with his hands at a trade.
> That was before he embarked on a new career, became active in the local community in his 30s, and then literally burst onto the scene as a candidate for his nation's highest

hope. He possessed a golden tongue and could talk to anyone and motivate them. He had a virtually nonexistent résumé, little work history, and no experience in leading a single organization. Yet he was a powerful speaker and citizens were drawn to him as though he were a magnet and they were small roofing tacks. He drew large crowds during public appearances and provided food for large groups of people. He attracted the lowest classes, and chose his closest followers, which included terrorists, traitors, sleazy business men, dockworkers, psychotics, hopelessly deranged outcasts, and prostitutes, over the rich, successful, and wealthy elite of society. At first, his public appearances focused on the needs of his countrymen, and he made many enemies among the powerful.

But soon, his rhetoric became so extreme that his own family thought he was insane and tried to get him to return home with them and abandon his crazy ideas. He was very critical of his country's leadership and its spiritual poverty, seizing every opportunity to call it, among other things, a bunch of snakes. The leaders soon began planning his death. He was launched into national prominence by being nominated for king, and yet, after a huge parade was thrown for him, walked away from the offer. He was the surprise candidate, emerging from outside the traditional path of politics and religion and was able to gain such widespread popular support that his enemies did not dare to touch him publicly.

He knew that he could change the world, and soon began to make speeches that openly suggested he was equal to God. Most of his followers deserted him because of this and other stances, such as his call for his followers to eat his flesh and drink his blood, and, in several incidents, others tried to stone him and to throw him over a cliff. His true views were not widely known, since he ordered his closest followers to keep them secret until after his death. He tried to keep his anger against the hypocrisy around him in check, but on two occasions, lost it, yelled, and publicly whipped a group of merchants. But, after his death, he became the most powerful being in the universe, and the world at last learned the truth of who had walked among them for three decades.

CHAPTER FIVE

DID PAUL "LOSE IT" IN GALATIANS 5:12?

All scripture is given by the inspiration of God.
— 2 Timothy 3:16

Be holy, for I the Lord am holy.
— Leviticus 19:2

Love your enemies.
— Luke 6:27

If you call someone Raca [worthless], you are in danger of hellfire.
— Matthew 5:22

Did Paul "Lose It" in Galatians 5:12?

I WORKED WITH THE LATE Ken Taylor during the process of transforming the Paraphrased Living Bible into the New Living Bible Translation, and during that time I made over six hundred suggestions on how a paraphrase could be made into a translation, much closer to the original manuscripts, and many of these were adopted. But astonishingly, the one verse I was never able to get them to change was Galatians 5:12. It seems that, in spite of the tenor of the rest of Paul's writing, and centuries of brilliant translators, and commentators who disagree with them, some translations still want to put cruel, vicious words in Paul's mouth.

Here is the verse in context:

> And I, brethren, if I still preach circumcision, why do I still suffer persecution? Then the offense of the cross has ceased. I could wish that those who trouble you would even cut

themselves off! For you, brethren, have been called to liberty; only do not use liberty as an opportunity for the flesh, but through love serve one another. (NKJV)

The problem comes when translators take the simple Greek word (*apokopto*) used in the New Testament only in Acts 27:32 where the soldiers cut off the ropes from the ship; (Apokopto= *apo* + *kopto*), and by Jesus, "If your right hand offends you, cut it off" (Mt. 5:30); and where Peter cut off the right ear of the High Priest's servant (Jn. 18:10). The term is clearly about cutting—but several modern translators have Paul wishing that those troubling the Galatians would—not "cut themselves off," that is, break fellowship—but, incredibly, to "castrate themselves," "mutilate themselves," or "emasculate themselves!"

First, we will look at some commentaries; then, we will investigate the origin of this monstrous idea.

> THEY . . . WHICH TROUBLE YOU—Translate, as the Greek is different from Galatians 5:10, "they who are *unsettling* you."
> WERE EVEN CUT OFF—even as they desire your foreskin to be *cut off* and cast away by circumcision, so would that *they were even cut off* from your communion, being worthless as a castaway foreskin (Gal. 1:7, 8; compare Phil. 3:2). The fathers—Jerome, Ambrose, Augustine, and Chrysostom—explain it, "Would that they would even cut themselves off," that is, cut off not merely the foreskin, but the whole member: if circumcision be not enough for them, then let them have *excision* also; an *outburst hardly suitable to the gravity of an apostle* [italics mine]. But Galatians 5:9-10 plainly points to excommunication as the judgment threatened against the troublers, and danger of the bad "leaven" spreading, as the reason for it (Jamieson, Fausset, and Brown).

Martin Luther's *Commentary on Galatians*:

Verse 12. I would they were even cut off which trouble you. *It hardly seems befitting an apostle*, [italics mine—but note the similarity to JFB] not only to denounce the false apostles as troublers of the Church, and to consign them to the devil, but also to wish that they were utterly cut off--what else would you call it but plain cursing? Paul, I suppose, is alluding to the rite of circumcision. As if he were saying to the Galatians: "The false apostles compel you to cut off the foreskin of your flesh. Well, I wish they themselves were utterly cut off by the roots. . . .

We had better answer at once the question, whether it is right for Christians to curse. Certainly not always, nor for every little cause. But when things have come to such a pass that God and his Word are openly blasphemed, then we must say: "Blessed be God and his Word, and cursed be everything that is contrary to God and His Word, even though it should be an apostle, or an angel from heaven. . . .

This goes to show again how much importance Paul attached to the least points of Christian doctrine, that he dared to curse the false apostles, evidently men of great popularity and influence. What right, then, have we to make little of doctrine? No matter how nonessential a point of doctrine may seem, if slighted it may prove the gradual disintegration of the truths of our salvation. . . .

Let us do everything to advance the glory and authority of God's Word. Every tittle of it is greater than heaven and earth. Christian charity and unity have nothing to do with (meaning: should not hold us back from defending) the Word of God. We are bold to curse and condemn all men who in the least point corrupt the Word of God, "for a little leaven leaveneth the whole lump."

Paul does right to curse these troublers of the Galatians, wishing that they were cut off and rooted out of the Church of God and that their doctrine might perish forever. Such cursing is the gift of the Holy Ghost. Thus Peter cursed Simon the sorcerer, "Thy money perish with thee." Many instances of this holy cursing are recorded in the sacred Scriptures, especially in the Psalms, e.g., "Let death seize upon them, and let them go down quick into hell." (Ps. 55:15.)[6]

Here are some of the English translations of the New Testament that I believe have followed both the Greek and the Holy Spirit:

> The 1599 Geneva Study Bible: I would they were even cut off which trouble you.
> KJV & NKJV: I would they were cut off from you who trouble you.
> The Douay-Rheims Bible: I would they were even cut off, who trouble you.
> The J.B. Rotherham Emphasized Bible: Oh! That they would even leave off in dismay, who are unsettling you!
> Young's Literal Translation: O that even they would cut themselves off who are unsettling you!
> The Latin Vulgate (425 AD): *Utinam et abscidantur qui vos conturbant* (O that even they might be cut off who trouble you).

******

Remember when I was discussing my difficulty with the New Living Translation? Here is how they translated Galatians 5:12: "I only wish that those troublemakers who want to mutilate you by circumcision would mutilate themselves." But what does the Greek say?

ofelon	*kai*	*apokoyontai*	*oi*	*anastatountev*	*umav.*
I would that	indeed	might cut themselves off	those	unsettling	you.

"I would that indeed, those who are unsettling you

might cut themselves off from you."

Do you see the problem? Here, at least, The New Living Translation is still a paraphrase, not a translation! There is nothing in the Greek about "troublemakers" or "mutilate" or "circumcision." How on earth did they get that from the Greek? Not even close!

Those with whom I corresponded at the NLB headquarters in Wheaton, IL, about changing their translation of this verse said that they were correct in their rendering, because of Greek scholars such as Joseph Thayer and Frederic Rendall. But these scholars go to the extreme of bringing in mythology to prove their point (their belief that Paul was suggesting mutilation or castration):

This word (*apokopto*) was habitually used to describe the practice of mutilation which was so prevalent in the Phrygian worship of Cybele. The Galatians were necessarily familiar with it, and it can hardly bear any other sense (Rendall).

Another "scholar" wrote:

> Finally, Paul wishes that those who demanded circumcision among the Gentiles would go all the way themselves, and amputate their genitalia altogether, not merely their foreskins. Sacred castration was known to citizens of the ancient world; it was frequently practiced by pagan priests in the cults in the region of Galatia. Paul's idea here is something like this: "If cutting will make you righteous, why don't you do like the pagan priests, go all the way and castrate yourself?" Morris rightly observes, "This was a dreadful thing to wish, but then the teaching was a dreadful thing to inflict on young Christians."

Thayer also wrote in his lexicon that the Sibylline

prophets mutilated themselves—as if that would influence Paul!

Think logically with me: Do you think the Holy Spirit would inspire Paul to write that he wished his enemies would mutilate, castrate, or emasculate themselves? No way.

CHAPTER SIX

DID PAUL WRITE THE BOOK OF HEBREWS?

Did Paul Write the Book of Hebrews?

SOME MODERN AUTHORS HAVE disputed it, promoting for their candidates such strange suggestions as Priscilla, Peter, Barnabas, Luke, Clement of Rome, and Apollos (Martin Luther's candidate).

But I think we can safely say, "Yes, Paul wrote Hebrews." Here is my reasoning:

> 1. The Amplified Bible translates 2 Thessalonians 3:17: "I, Paul, write you this final greeting with my own hand. This is the mark and sign [that it is not a forgery] in every letter of mine. It is the way I write [my handwriting and signature]."
>
> Paul wanted to assure his readers that each of his letters was indeed written by him (though often dictated to a scribe or amanuensis). There was always a personal signature at the end of each epistle. He also concluded

each epistle with a blessing—every single one of which contains the word grace—including Hebrews:

Romans 16:24—The GRACE of our Lord Jesus Christ be WITH you all. Amen.

1 Corinthians 16:23—The GRACE of our Lord Jesus Christ be WITH you.

2 Corinthians 13:14—The GRACE of the Lord Jesus Christ . . . be WITH you all. Amen.

Galatians 6:18—Brethren, the GRACE of our Lord Jesus Christ be WITH your spirit. Amen.

Ephesians 6:24—GRACE WITH all them that love our Lord Jesus Christ in sincerity. Amen.

Philippians 4:23—The GRACE of our Lord Jesus Christ be WITH you all. Amen.

Colossians 4:18—The salutation by the hand of me, Paul . . . GRACE be WITH you. Amen.

1 Thessalonians 5:28—The GRACE of our Lord Jesus Christ be WITH you. Amen.

2 Thessalonians 3:18—The GRACE of our Lord Jesus Christ be WITH you all. Amen.

1 Timothy 6:21—GRACE be WITH you. Amen.

2 Timothy 4:22—GRACE be WITH you. Amen.

Titus 3:15—GRACE be WITH you all. Amen.

Philemon 1:25—The GRACE of our Lord Jesus Christ be WITH your spirit. Amen.

Hebrews 13:25—GRACE be WITH you all. Amen.

2. In Hebrews we find the clear relationship between the writer and Timothy, whom Paul calls "my own son in the faith," "son Timothy," and "my dearly beloved son" (1 Tim. 1:2, and 1:18; 2 Tim 2:1). The author of Hebrews writes, "Take notice that our brother Timothy has been released, with whom, if he comes soon, I will see you" (Heb. 13:23, NAS). Coincidence? Some other author who also happens to know Timothy? Unlikely.

Except for three mentions of Timothy in the book of Acts, no one in the rest of the New Testament ever mentions Timothy except Paul, and he refers to him seventeen times!

3. The King James Version of 1611 has as the heading to Hebrews: "The Epistle of Paul the Apostle to the Hebrews." This was not questioned by the early church fathers and most early commentaries. The church in the fourth century, affirmed by no less than Augustine and Jerome, deemed that Hebrews was the fourteenth epistle of Paul. This was commonly agreed to until the time of the Reformation.

4. Some commentaries and writers have denied Paul's authorship of Hebrews based on the difference in style found in Hebrews as compared to Paul's other epistles. I agree—the style is different. But this certainly does not prove that Paul was not the author of Hebrews. Paul was a self-described "Hebrew born of Hebrews" (Phil. 3:5); his training, background, and culture was Jewish. He loved God's people so much that he stated he could wish himself accursed from Christ if it would mean salvation for his people, the Jews (Rom. 9:3, passim). Therefore, if Paul wanted to write an epistle specifically targeting people raised in the Jewish faith (Hebrews), he would do so without throwing the fact that he was the apostle to the Gentiles in their face. He would write in the style of a Jew, not in the style he would use in writing to Gentiles. He would approach Jews by reminding them of their past, about their covenant with God, and about their patriarchs and the prophets of the Old Testament.

That is exactly what he did in Hebrews 1:1, beginning: "God, after He spoke long ago to the fathers (patriarchs) in the prophets in many portions and in many ways . . ." (NAS). He wrote to them about the ways in which *Yeshua Hamashiach* (Hebrew for Jesus the Messiah) fulfilled every promise in the Old Testament. He described how the temple, the sacrifices, and the Ark of the Covenant all pointed to Jesus. Thus, yes, the style is indeed different from Paul's other epistles and deliberately so.

Unless someone discovers the original (called an "autograph," or self-written) copy of the epistle to the Hebrews, signed by Paul, we may never be able to prove definitively whether or not he wrote it. But I think there is ample evidence to indicate his authorship.

CHAPTER SEVEN

WHAT WAS PAUL'S THORN IN THE FLESH?

Paul writes in 2 Corinthians 12:7-10:

> And lest I should be exalted above measure by the abundance of the revelations, a thorn in the flesh was given to me, a *messenger of Satan* to buffet me, lest I be exalted above measure. Concerning this thing I pleaded with the Lord three times that it might depart from me. And He said to me, "My grace is sufficient for you, for my strength is made perfect in weakness." Therefore most gladly I will rather boast in my *infirmities*, that the power of Christ may rest upon me. Therefore I take pleasure in *infirmities*, in *reproaches*, in *needs*, in *persecutions*, in *distresses*, for Christ's sake. For when I am weak, then I am strong (my italics, emphasizing what forms the "thorn" took).

Paul describes it for us so plainly that we cannot miss it: what was his thorn in the flesh? It was a messenger of Satan. The Greek word for messenger is *angelos* (angel). It is apparently clear that God assigned a specific spirit to buffet Paul—and everywhere Paul went, it seemed there was a riot stirred up by this evil spirit. But Paul also had a physical affliction, and what form the thorn in his *flesh* took is hinted at in Galatians 4:13-15:

> You know that because of *physical infirmity* I preached the gospel to you at the first. And my trial, which was in my flesh, you did not despise or reject, but you received me as an angel of God, even as Christ Jesus. What then was the blessing you enjoyed? For I bear you witness that, if possible, you would have *plucked out your own eyes* and given them to me.

This indicates that Paul may have had an infirmity of some kind in his eyes. Not only were diseases of the eye common in the Middle East, but it has also been speculated that the injury done to Paul when they stoned him and dragged out of the city "supposing him to be dead" (Acts 14:19) may have resulted in permanent damage to his eyes, even near-blindness. This is further supported by his cryptic remark later in the same epistle (Gal. 6:11): "See with what large letters I have written to you with my own hand." It would explain why he used a scribe—if his eyesight was so bad he had to write in large letters, given the cost of paper, he would have had to employ an amanuensis to write for him.

CHAPTER EIGHT

FINAL THOUGHT

W E ONLY SEE "THROUGH A glass darkly" all that Jesus Christ has accomplished by His death and resurrection. He had unbroken fellowship with the Father and with the Spirit from eons uncounted. The three members of the Godhead existed from eternity, needing nothing. But being, as to Their very essence, *agapē* love, They desired to share that love with beings that would freely choose to love Them in return. They created a universe filled with four billion trillion stars, and a universe of scintillating beauty that included millions of galaxies, nebulae, and planets. They enjoyed their creation for eons uncounted, wandering among sights no mortal can imagine. The members of the Godhead existed in a state of timeless love, one for the other. The Father loved the Son, and the Spirit loved the Son, and in Their mind, from the beginning, They planned a way of showing how much They loved Him.

There was to be a royal wedding, and the Son was to marry a bride without spot or wrinkle. But first, there must be a companion fit for the Son of God. So They fashioned the human race, such that each individual would compose the "cells" of her body—millions and millions of tiny images of God, fragments of the complete image of God. The cells all had free will, and could choose whether or not to participate. Many chose not to join together, but many did.

The Son had to come into the world and inhabit a body like those He had created. He had to lay aside his glory, power, and the attributes of deity; become one of the cells; take on their sins; die a painful death; and rise again. It was imperative that He do this in order to conquer the virus of death that infected the "cells" of the bride's body—a virus that had been inherited from the Sin of the first man and woman. The Godhead purposed that the Son would someday return and claim His bride.

Jesus prayed, "Holy Father, keep through Your name those whom You have given Me, that they may be one as We are, that they all may be one, as You, Father, are in Me, and I in You; *that they also may be one in Us . . .*" (Jn. 17:11 & 21, emphasis mine)

The cells are not God, individually, coming far short of His awesome power; yet, taken all together, they will make up a being that seems destined to enter the Godhead as a fourth member. The mystery is that the members of the bride are also spoken of as "many members" of the Body of Christ, as He is its head.

Peter described it in a similar manner, using the simile of individual stones that make up the temple of God: "You also, as living stones, are being built up a spiritual house, a

Final Thought

holy priesthood, to offer up spiritual sacrifices acceptable to God through Jesus Christ" (1 Pt. 2:5).

And John wrote: "And then one of the seven angels . . . came to me and talked with me, saying, 'Come, I will show you the bride, the Lamb's wife'" (Rev. 21:9).

And one day when "the Spirit and the bride say, "Come!" (Rev. 22:17), the Son will return for His bride, and the two shall be One for all eternity with the Father and the Spirit.

APPENDIX

MORE FROM MILTON

It is interesting to note how much Milton added to the Word of God (as have many contemporary authors we could name) putting words into God's own mouth! From Book 7, again:

> "Know then, that, after Lucifer from heav'n
> (So call him, brighter once amidst the host
> Of angels, than that star the stars among)
> Fell with his flaming legions through the deep
> Into his place, and the great Son returned
> Victorious with his saints, th' Omnipotent
> Eternal Father from his throne beheld
> Their multitude, and to his Son thus spake.
>   "'At least our envious foe hath failed, who thought
> All like himself rebellious, by whose aid
> This inaccessible high strength, the seat
> Of Deity supreme, us dispossessed,
> He trusted to have seized, and into fraud

> Drew many, whom their place knows here no more;
> Yet far the greater part have kept, I see,
> Their station, heav'n yet populous retains
> Number sufficient to possess her realms
> Though wide, and this high temple to frequent
> With ministeries due and solemn rites:
> But lest his heart exalt him in the harm
> Already done, to have dispeopled heav'n,
> My damage fondly deemed, I can repair
> That detriment, if such it be to lose
> Self-lost, and in a moment will create
> Another world, out of one man a race
> Of men innumerable, there to dwell,
> Not here, till by degrees of merit raised
> They open to themselves at length the way
> Up hither, under long obedience tried,
> And earth be changed to heav'n, and heav'n to earth,
> One kingdom, joy and union without end.' "[8]

Interesting as poetry, but containing a great deal of speculation about Satan. Most Christians would say that they have always believed something similar to what Milton penned, but a careful study of the scriptures reveals that it is just not true.

NOTES

1. C. S. Lewis, Mere Christianity (New York: Macmillan, 1943), 55-56.
2. *Amplified Bible* (Grand Rapids: Zondervan, 1974), 777.
3. G. R. Evans, *Augustine On Evil* (Cambridge: Cambridge University Press, 1982), 99.
4. There is considerable debate on what Luther might actually have said. Some reports, notably the *Weimarkritisches Gesamtausgabe* and the American edition of Luther's works (Philadelphia: Muelenberg/Fortress Press and St. Louis: Concordia) attribute to Luther, »*Der Teufel ist Gottes Affe*«—"The devil is God's ape." What he actually spoke at table we most likely will never know for certain.
5. G. R. Evans, op. cit.
6. Augustine, *Enchiridion*, http://www.intratext.com/ixt/eng0135/_p3.htm.
7. http://www.studylight.org/com/mlg/view.cgi?book=ga&chapter=005
8. John Milton, *Paradise Lost*. Ed. by Scott Elledge (New York: W. W. Norton, 1993), 166-167.

BIBLIOGRAPHY

The Amplified Bible, Grand Rapids: Zondervan, 1974.
Biblia Sacra, iuxta vulgata versionem, trans. by St. Jerome, Stuttgart: Deutsche Bibelgesellschaft, Stuttgart, 1983.
Evans, G. R. *Augustine On Evil*, Cambridge: Cambridge University Press, 1982.
Jamieson, Robert, A.R. Fausset, and David Brown. *Commentary Practical and Explanatory on the Whole Bible*, Grand Rapids: Zondervan, 1982.
Lewis, C. S. *Mere Christianity*. New York: Macmillan, 1943.
Luther, Martin. *Commentary on Galatians*. Http://www.studylight.org/com/mlg/view.cgi?book=ga&chapter=005.
Milton, John. *Paradise Lost*. Edited by Scott Elledge. New York: W. W. Norton, 1993.
Morris, William & Mary, *Dictionary of Word and Phrase Origins*, New York: Harper & Row, 1998.

YOU MIGHT WISH TO MAKE NOTES OF YOUR OWN DISCOVERIES HERE

www.ingramcontent.com/pod-product-compliance
Lightning Source LLC
Chambersburg PA
CBHW021014090426
42738CB00007B/782